You will never have to search very far for me,
because I am always with you.
I am the twinkle in the stars and the chirp of
the bird outside your window.
I am the love in your heart.
When you are missing me
simply say my name and I will be with you.

This book is dedicated to you, our sweet Dad,
our gentle and loving Poppy.
Wherever you may be now, this book brings
you back to us.
In every word, in every dream. In our hearts
you will always be.

Copyright © 2021 Heather Eimers
All rights reserved.

Emotions are feelings, things you can't see.

From inside your heart, right down to your knees.

Emotions are when you are happy or sad, when you are confused and when you are mad.

Then there is the one you may not <u>have</u> felt yet.
The one we call grief, the one we forget.

Grief is like sadness; it fits like a glove when we can no longer see somebody we love.

One day you look around and something feels wrong.
All of a sudden a loved one is gone.

Everyone around you is suddenly sad, maybe your grandparent, your mom or your dad.

Grief feels like a hurt deep inside your heart, when you and somebody you love are apart.

At first grief will feel tough to understand. It will follow you around and may not go as planned.

Some days will feel good and some days will feel hard. Some days all you'll feel is exhausted and tired.

Grief often feels lonely but you are not alone.
Grief is an emotion that many friends know.
A friend like a neighbour or maybe a teacher.
Don't forget that your friends will be there if you need them.

It will even be okay if you're angry and don't know why.

When someone you love can no longer be seen, until suddenly one night they come in a dream.

They call out your name and hold on to you tight. Maybe they say nothing but every thing will feel right.

You may start to see the things that they loved, and smile while you think of a thing that once was.

Something as simple as a song they would play, a drink they would drink or a word they would say.

You'll remember the joy they brought to your life, the things that they taught you and things that feel bright.

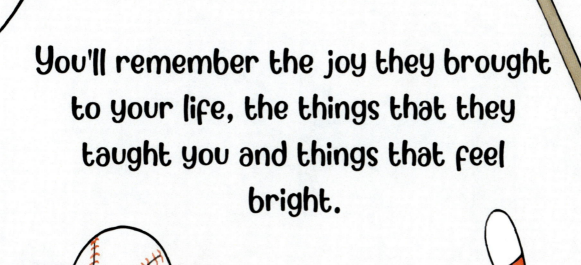

So the next time grief creeps in and things start to feel heavy, just close your eyes and when you are ready....

Take a deep breath and remember the good.

Grief will take time to heal as it should.

They are with you in spirit, memory and heart, and as long as you remember you will never be apart.

Until we meet again……..

Manufactured by Amazon.ca
Bolton, ON